# The Legacy and Legend of Sacagawea

Margaret King

## Consultants

**Vanessa Ann Gunther, Ph.D.**
Department of History
Chapman University

**Nicholas Baker, Ed.D.**
Supervisor of Curriculum and Instruction
Colonial School District, DE

**Katie Blomquist, Ed.S.**
Fairfax County Public Schools

## Publishing Credits

Rachelle Cracchiolo, M.S.Ed., *Publisher*
Conni Medina, M.A.Ed., *Managing Editor*
Emily R. Smith, M.A.Ed., *Series Developer*
Diana Kenney, M.A.Ed., NBCT, *Content Director*
Courtney Patterson, *Senior Graphic Designer*
Lynette Ordoñez, *Editor*

**Image Credits:** Cover and p. 1 Robert Bird/Alamy Stock Photo; p. 5 Courtesy of the Montana Historical Society, X1912.07.01; pp. 7, 26-27 Granger, NYC; p. 8 Library of Congress/Wikimedia Commons; p. 9 (top) Gerry Embleton/North Wind Picture Archives, (bottom) Detail, E.S. Paxson, Lewis and Clark's Camp at Traveler's Rest, 1805, oil on linen, 1914, 68" x 122". Courtesy of Missoula County and Missoula Art Museum; p. 10 (left) Courtesy of the Diplomatic Reception Rooms, U.S. Department of State, (right) Record Group 233, Records of the United States House of Representatives, HR 7A-D1; National Archives; p. 11 National Gallery of Art; pp. 12, 16 (back), 29, 32 North Wind Picture Archives; p. 14 (left) Nancy Carter/North Wind Picture Archives, (right) Courtesy of the Montana Historical Society, X1912.07.01; p. 15 George Ostertag/Alamy Stock Photo; p. 16 (front) Witold Skrypczak/Alamy Stock Photo; p. 17 Dennis Macdonald/Getty Images; p. 19 (right) Everett Collection Inc/Alamy Stock Photo; pp. 18-19 Lewis and Clark Reach Shoshone Camp Led by Sacajawea the "Bird Woman" (1918), Oil on canvas. Overall: 36 3/4 × 54 3/4 × 3 in. (93.3 × 139.1 × 7.6 cm), Image: 29 1/2 × 47 1/2 in. (74.9 × 120.7 cm), GM 0137.2267, Gilcrease Museum, Tulsa, Oklahoma; p. 20 Illustration by Michael Haynes; p. 21 E.S. Paxson, Lewis and Clark's Camp at Traveler's Rest, 1805, oil on linen, 1914, 68" x 122". Courtesy of Missoula County and Missoula Art Museum; p. 22 Lowell Georgia/Getty Images; p. 23 (top) Fort Clatsop National Memorial Collection FOCL 000104 Cat. No. 698, (bottom) Library of Congress/Internet Archive; p. 24 Wood Ronsaville Harlin, Inc. USA/Bridgeman Images; p. 25 (top) Vespasian/Alamy Stock Photo, (bottom) Luc Novovitch/Alamy Stock Photo; p. 31 Joseph Sohm/Shutterstock.com; all other images from iStock and/or Shutterstock.

### Library of Congress Cataloging-in-Publication Data

Names: King, Margaret (Margaret Esther), author.
Title: The legacy and legend of Sacagawea / Margaret King.
Description: Huntington Beach, CA : Teacher Created Materials, [2016] | Includes index. | Audience: Grades 4-6.
Identifiers: LCCN 2016034136 (print) | LCCN 2016036587 (ebook) | ISBN 9781493837939 (pbk.) | ISBN 9781480757585 (eBook)
Subjects: LCSH: Sacagawea--Juvenile literature. | Shoshoni women--Biography--Juvenile literature. | Shoshoni Indians--Juvenile literature. | Lewis and Clark Expedition (1804-1806)--Juvenile literature.
Classification: LCC F592.7.S123 K55 2016 (print) | LCC F592.7.S123 (ebook) | DDC 978.004/9745740092 [B] --dc23
LC record available at https://lccn.loc.gov/2016034136

### Teacher Created Materials

5301 Oceanus Drive
Huntington Beach, CA 92649-1030
http://www.tcmpub.com

**ISBN 978-1-4938-3793-9**

# Table of Contents

# The Woman Behind the Legend

U.S. coins usually honor the Founding Fathers and great presidents. The quarter shows George Washington. The nickel honors Thomas Jefferson. The face on the penny is Abraham Lincoln. But in 2000, the United States minted a dollar coin with the face of a teenage American Indian. Her name was Sacagawea.

How did this teenager earn an honor that is normally reserved for the nation's leaders? Sacagawea joined Lewis and Clark's famous **expedition**. Together the group explored a vast new part of the country. They paved the way for Americans to move west. Sacagawea joined them as an **interpreter**. She went with Lewis and Clark every step of the hard, dangerous journey. And she made this amazing trip with her infant son on her back.

Time after time, Sacagawea helped the explorers. Her life inspired legends. This is the story of the woman behind the legend.

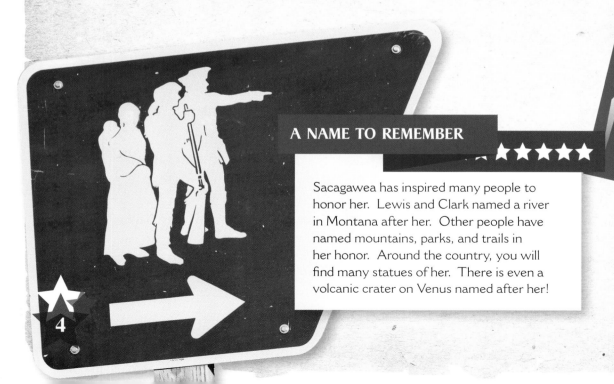

## A NAME TO REMEMBER

★★★★★

Sacagawea has inspired many people to honor her. Lewis and Clark named a river in Montana after her. Other people have named mountains, parks, and trails in her honor. Around the country, you will find many statues of her. There is even a volcanic crater on Venus named after her!

Sacagawea with Lewis and Clark

Sacagawea dollar coin

LIBERTY

IN GOD WE TRUST

5

# Growing Up

We know very little about Sacagawea's childhood. She was born into the Lemhi **band** of the Shoshone (shuh-SHO-nee) Indian **tribe** around 1788. Her village was in the Rocky Mountains near what is now Idaho. The Lemhi had never seen white people. The band did not have guns. The men hunted buffalo, elk, and bears with bows and arrows. The band had strong horses that moved easily over the harsh **terrain**. These horses would play an important role in the journey of Lewis and Clark.

Sawtooth range of the Rocky Mountains in Idaho

## HOW DO YOU SAY IT?

Sacagawea's name means either "bird woman" or "boat puller." In their journals, Lewis and Clark spelled her name many different ways, but they always wrote it with a *g*. Many **historians** think her name should be pronounced that way—sah–kuh–guh–WEE–uh.

As a girl in the Lemhi band, Sacagawea worked hard. Women and girls collected fruit, seeds, and roots to eat. They cared for the horses, set up **tepees**, and sewed clothing. After visiting the Lemhi, Lewis wrote that they "treat their women but with little respect, and compel them to perform every species of drudgery."

During the harsh winters, the band stayed in valleys of the Rocky Mountains. They bundled up to keep warm. When the days grew warmer, they traveled to a place called Three Forks in what is now Montana to find buffalo. It was during one of these trips that Sacagawea's life changed forever.

Shoshone village in Wyoming

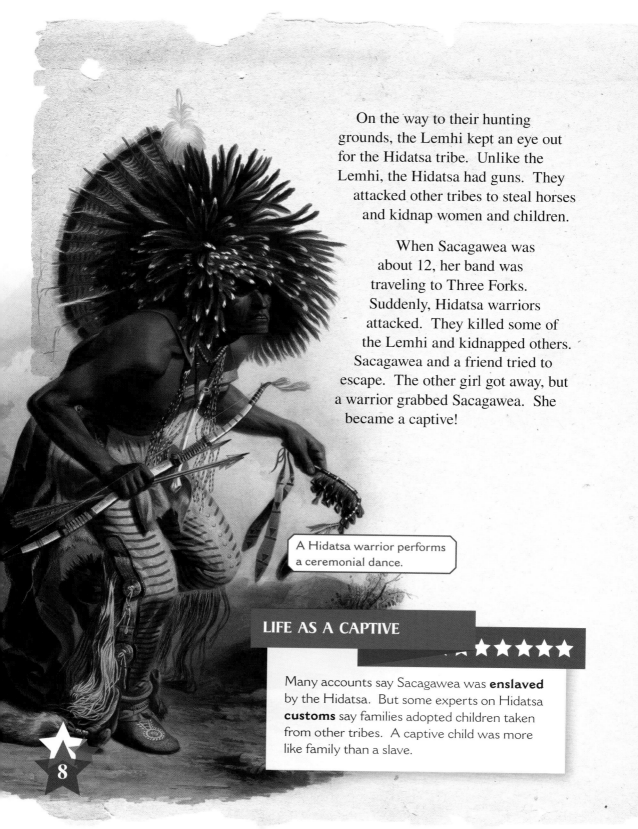

On the way to their hunting grounds, the Lemhi kept an eye out for the Hidatsa tribe. Unlike the Lemhi, the Hidatsa had guns. They attacked other tribes to steal horses and kidnap women and children.

When Sacagawea was about 12, her band was traveling to Three Forks. Suddenly, Hidatsa warriors attacked. They killed some of the Lemhi and kidnapped others. Sacagawea and a friend tried to escape. The other girl got away, but a warrior grabbed Sacagawea. She became a captive!

A Hidatsa warrior performs a ceremonial dance.

## LIFE AS A CAPTIVE

★★★★★

Many accounts say Sacagawea was **enslaved** by the Hidatsa. But some experts on Hidatsa **customs** say families adopted children taken from other tribes. A captive child was more like family than a slave.

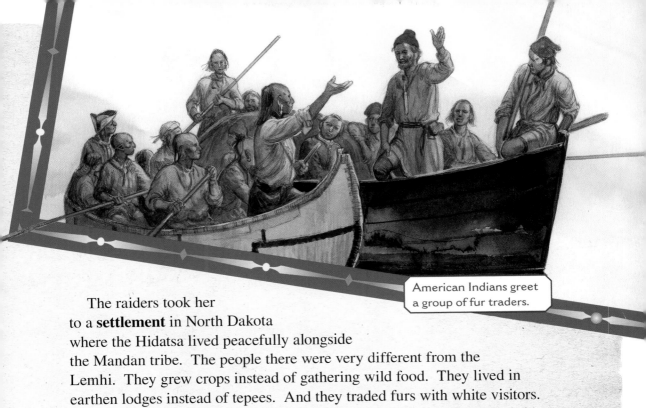

American Indians greet a group of fur traders.

The raiders took her to a **settlement** in North Dakota where the Hidatsa lived peacefully alongside the Mandan tribe. The people there were very different from the Lemhi. They grew crops instead of gathering wild food. They lived in earthen lodges instead of tepees. And they traded furs with white visitors. Sacagawea may have tended crops or sewed clothes for the tribe. And she learned to speak the Hidatsa language.

A French Canadian fur trader named Toussaint Charbonneau (too-SAHN SHAR-boh-no) lived nearby. When Sacagawea was about 15, he bought her from the Hidatsa. He took her and another Shoshone woman as his wives. Sacagawea went to live with the fur trader, who was at least 20 years older than her. Her life was about to change again.

## MANY WIVES

★★★★★

According to tribal **lore**, Charbonneau's other wife was named Otter Woman. Over the years he had other American Indian wives. In many tribes, it was an accepted custom for a man to have more than one wife.

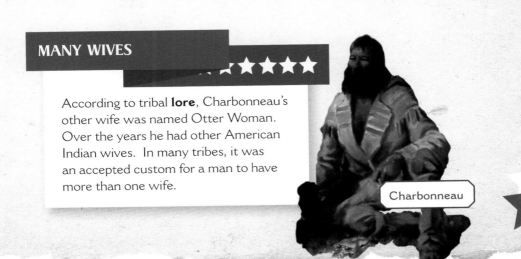

Charbonneau

9

# Opening the West

While Sacagawea was living among her captors, big events were taking place. France got a large piece of land in North America from Spain in 1800. It was called the Louisiana **Territory**. President Thomas Jefferson worried that France would close the port of New Orleans. Americans needed to use the port. So, he sent negotiators to Paris in 1803. Their job was to make a deal to buy New Orleans. But they got a big surprise. The French offered to sell the whole Louisiana Territory! The Louisiana Purchase included land from the Mississippi River to the Rocky Mountains and north to Canada.

The Americans quickly agreed. They only paid about three cents per acre of land. The deal doubled the size of the young country. It opened the West for exploration.

What was in this vast new territory? Jefferson decided to send an expedition to find out. He wanted to map the land. He hoped to find the Northwest Passage, a fabled water route to the Pacific Ocean. And he wanted to tell the American Indian tribes that they were now living on U.S. lands. He knew just the man for the job.

In this letter, Jefferson asks Congress for money to explore the Louisiana Territory.

Thomas Jefferson

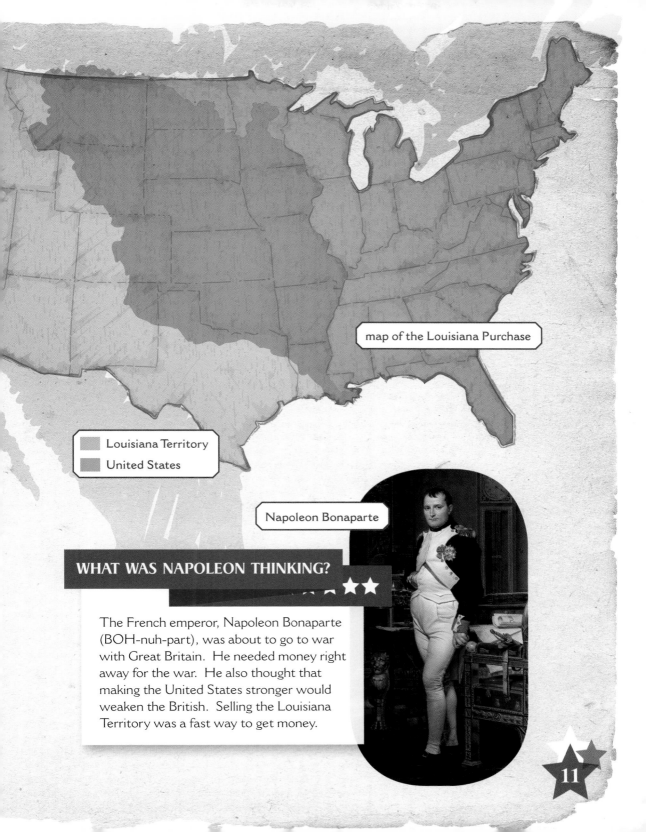

map of the Louisiana Purchase

Louisiana Territory
United States

Napoleon Bonaparte

## WHAT WAS NAPOLEON THINKING?

The French emperor, Napoleon Bonaparte (BOH-nuh-part), was about to go to war with Great Britain. He needed money right away for the war. He also thought that making the United States stronger would weaken the British. Selling the Louisiana Territory was a fast way to get money.

Jefferson's personal secretary and right-hand man was Meriwether Lewis. Jefferson chose Lewis to lead the expedition to explore the new territory. Lewis asked his friend William Clark to be co-leader. The two men had served in the army together. Lewis was 29 years old and Clark was 33.

Meriwether Lewis

William Clark

## WRITTEN RECORD

★ ★ ★ ★

Lewis and Clark kept detailed journals of their trip. They described landscapes, American Indian tribes, and plants and animals they saw along the way. Their journals gave Americans their first look at the West. And they gave us most of what we know about Sacagawea.

pages from Clark's journal

Lewis and Clark were alike in some ways. They were both over six feet tall, strong, and fit. Both were army officers who had spent time on the **frontier**. They were both brave, loyal, and had proven to be good leaders.

In other ways, they were very different. Lewis was more educated. He had a gift for observing and describing things. But he was impulsive and moody. Clark was more levelheaded and practical. He had a warm and easy way with people.

Lewis and Clark recruited soldiers, sailors, and hunters to join their crew. Lewis even brought his dog, Seaman. They called themselves the **Corps** (KOHR) of Discovery. In May of 1804, the Corps left St. Louis with about 45 members. They traveled up the Missouri River in canoes and flat-bottomed sailboats. One place they planned to stop was the Hidatsa and Mandan settlement in North Dakota.

This is a replica of a keelboat, similar to what Lewis and Clark used.

# The Journey Begins

The Corps of Discovery arrived at the Hidatsa and Mandan settlement in October of 1804. Lewis and Clark met tribal chiefs and gave them gifts. In return, the chiefs offered them corn and buffalo meat. Lewis and Clark decided to spend the winter there. They built eight cabins with a wall around them. They called their shelter Fort Mandan.

Charbonneau, the fur trader, came to see Lewis and Clark. He told them he could speak Hidatsa. He said he had a wife who could speak Hidatsa and Shoshone. He offered their services as interpreters. Lewis and Clark knew they would need horses to cross the Rocky Mountains. They hoped to trade with the Shoshone to get those horses. So, they agreed to Charbonneau's offer.

replica of Fort Mandan

Charbonneau

Charbonneau brought Sacagawea to meet Lewis and Clark. They soon learned some surprising news—she was pregnant! She gave birth in Fort Mandan on February 11, 1805. She named her son Jean Baptiste (ZHAHN BAP-teest).

On April 7, 1805, the Corps of Discovery set sail up the Missouri River. Some men had been sent home for misbehaving and other reasons. One man had died from an infection. So the Corps now had 33 members, including Sacagawea and her two-month-old son. She would have to carry him the whole way. Many believe she put him in a **cradleboard** on her back.

statue of Sacagawea with Jean Baptiste in a cradleboard

## NAMES AMONG FRIENDS

★★★★★

Clark was especially fond of Sacagawea's son, Jean Baptiste. He called the boy Pomp or Pompey. Clark even named a rock formation in Montana Pompey's Tower. Today it's called Pompey's Pillar.

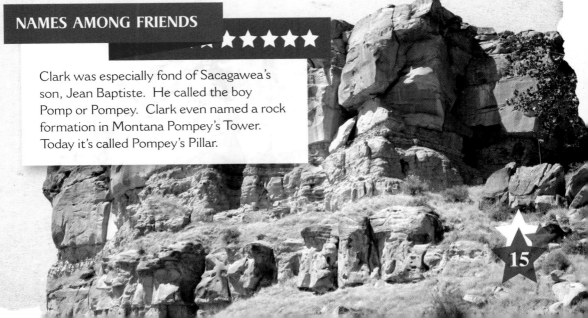

15

Great Falls, Montana

This diorama depicts the Corps moving a canoe over land to avoid a waterfall.

The Corps traveled against the Missouri River's current. Sometimes, the men had to wade into the icy water to push the boats. Sacagawea walked alongside the boats for miles while carrying her son. She always did her part to help the travelers. Along the way, she found berries and roots for them to eat.

One day, Sacagawea got a chance to help even more. A gust of wind hit the boat she and her husband were in. The boat tipped and started to fill with water. Charbonneau yelled for help. From the shore, Lewis and Clark saw that a few men were bailing water out of the boat. Then, they noticed something else. Still holding her baby, Sacagawea was calmly gathering papers and tools that had washed overboard. She saved many important items. Lewis and Clark were impressed. Lewis wrote in his journal that Sacagawea had "equal fortitude and resolution" to anyone on the boat.

In June of 1805, Sacagawea became ill with a high fever. Lewis and Clark cared for her until she felt better. There was more trouble ahead, though. The travelers came to a magnificent series of waterfalls. They had to carry their boats over land. It took a month of pushing, pulling, and lifting to get the boats around the falls.

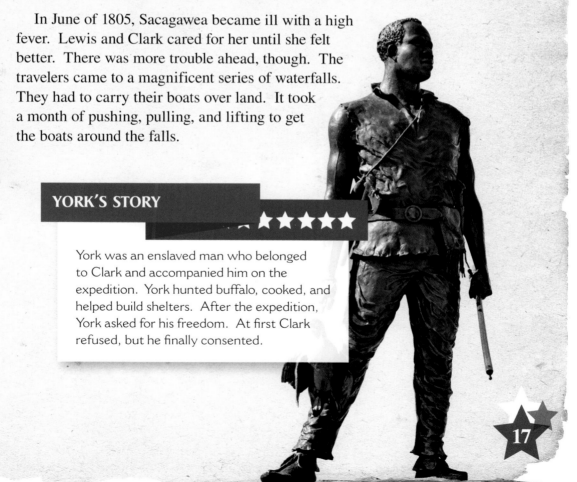

## YORK'S STORY

★★★★★

York was an enslaved man who belonged to Clark and accompanied him on the expedition. York hunted buffalo, cooked, and helped build shelters. After the expedition, York asked for his freedom. At first Clark refused, but he finally consented.

# A Joyful Reunion

After crossing the waterfalls, the travelers went on by boat. They reached the Three Forks area of Montana. In late July of 1805, Sacagawea was walking on the riverbank alongside the boats. She realized she knew this place—it was where she had been kidnapped! Lewis and Clark were excited by this news. They had reached Shoshone land, where they hoped to trade for horses.

Lewis went ahead on foot with three men while the others followed in boats. Lewis's group found some Shoshone women, who took them to their camp. The Shoshone chief, Cameahwait (cuh-MEE-uh-wait), greeted Lewis warmly.

Lewis persuaded some of the Shoshone to accompany him to a river fork to meet the Corps of Discovery. But when they got to the river, the boats were not there. The Shoshone grew suspicious. Was this an ambush?

Finally, the boats arrived. When Sacagawea saw the Shoshone, she realized something amazing—it was her own Lemhi band! She danced for joy. In the Lemhi camp, a young woman rushed toward her. It was the girl who had escaped from the Hidatsa raiders when Sacagawea was kidnapped. The two friends hugged. But an even bigger surprise awaited Sacagawea.

## WELCOME TO AMERICA!

A key part of Lewis and Clark's mission was letting the tribes know they now lived in part of the United States. Lewis and Clark explained to the leaders of each tribe that Jefferson was their new "great father." They gave gifts to the chiefs, including medals with Jefferson's face.

Thomas Jefferson's "Indian Peace Medal"

Sacagawea is reunited with her Lemhi band.

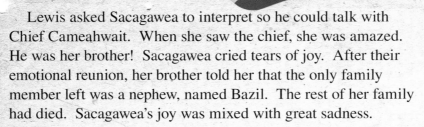

Lewis asked Sacagawea to interpret so he could talk with Chief Cameahwait. When she saw the chief, she was amazed. He was her brother! Sacagawea cried tears of joy. After their emotional reunion, her brother told her that the only family member left was a nephew, named Bazil. The rest of her family had died. Sacagawea's joy was mixed with great sadness.

The talks began. Lewis was still hoping to find a water route to the Pacific Ocean, but Cameahwait told him that the only way to get there was to cross the Rocky Mountains. The chief agreed to provide horses for the trip. In return, Cameahwait wanted guns so the Lemhi could fight their enemies and hunt more easily. Lewis promised he would send guns.

Sacagawea shows Chief Cameahwait his nephew, Jean Baptiste.

view of the Rocky Mountains from Bitterroot Valley, Montana

20

The Corps rests before continuing on their journey.

After a few days, Sacagawea said good-bye to her band. The Corps of Discovery started over the mountains with 29 horses, one mule, and a Shoshone guide named Old Toby. The trip was incredibly difficult. The horses slipped on the steep rocks. The men were hungry and bitterly cold. Many of them became sick.

In late September of 1805, they finally made it through the mountains. A friendly band of Nez Percé (PUHRS) Indians gave them fish and bread to eat. The Nez Percé had good news for the travelers—they were getting close to the Pacific Ocean.

## TRANSLATION CHAIN

To **translate** between Lewis and the Lemhi chief, the chief first spoke in Shoshone. Sacagawea translated his message into Hidatsa. Then, Charbonneau translated it to French. Finally, a French member of the Corps translated it to English so Lewis could understand it.

SHOSHONE → HIDATSA → FRENCH → ENGLISH

# The Road Home

The Nez Percé showed the visitors how to hollow out logs with fire to make canoes. With five new canoes, the explorers went on by water to the Columbia River. The Nez Percé agreed to care for the Corps' horses until the travelers returned.

On November 24, 1805, the Corps voted on where to build a winter camp. Sacagawea and York were both allowed to cast votes. The group built a shelter called Fort Clatsop near what is now Astoria, Oregon. They spent a rainy, miserable winter there.

In January of 1806, the Corps heard reports that a dead whale had washed ashore. Clark decided to take some men to the Pacific Ocean to get the whale's blubber. Sacagawea asked if she could come along. The trip took two days. The whale's bones were already picked clean, but the Corps traded with a local tribe for blubber and oil. And Sacagawea saw the vast Pacific Ocean.

In March, the Corps of Discovery headed home. With the help of Nez Percé guides, they made it through the mountains much faster than before. Lewis and Clark split the Corps into two groups to learn more about the land.

These men demonstrate how the Corps carved logs into canoes.

Sacagawea helps the Corps trade with local tribes at Fort Clatsop.

## 54 LEWIS AND CLARKE'S EXPEDITION.

the rapid before any, except one of the small canoes, he sat down on a rock to wait for them, and, seeing a crane fly across the river, shot it, and it fell near him. Several Indians had been before this passing on the opposite side towards the rapids, and some who were then nearly in front of him, being either alarmed at his appearance or the report of the gun, fled to their houses. G... Clarke was afr... these people...

## SINGULAR BELIEF OF THE INDIANS. 55

the houses, he seated himself on a rock, and beckoned to some of the men to come and smoke with him; but none of them ventured to join him till the canoes arrived with the two chiefs, who immediately explained our pacific intention towards them. Soon after the interpreter's wife landed, and her presence dissipated all doubts of our being well-disposed, since in this country no woman ever accompanies a war party; they therefore all came out, and seemed perfectly reconciled; nor could we, indeed, blame them for their terrors, which were perfectly natural. They told the two chiefs that they knew we were not men, for they had seen us fall from the clouds. In fact, Captain Clarke had seen the duck which he had shot fall, and as there was no other movement, they con... sudden appear... actually dropped from the clouds; considering the noise of the rifle, which they had never heard before, the sound announcing so extraordinary an event. This belief was strengthened, when, on entering the room, he brought down fire from the heavens by means of his burning-glass. We soon convinced them, however, that we were merely mortals; and after one of our chiefs had explained our history and objects, we all smoked together in great harmony. These people do not speak precisely the same language as the Indians farther up, but understand them in conversation. In a short time we were joined by many of the inhabitants from below, several of them on horseb... pleased to see us, and to exch... ries for a few trink...

### KEEPING THE PEACE ★★★★★

Almost all the meetings between the Corps and American Indian groups were peaceful. When tribes saw a woman with the Corps, they knew the visitors came in peace. Lewis wrote that in American Indian **culture**, "no woman ever accompanies a war party."

1868 book about Lewis and Clark's expedition

...to visit a house, he entered each of his ...this house, and directing each of his he found the inmates more terrified than those in the first; but he succeeded in pacifying them, and afterward went into the other houses, where the men had been equally successful. Retiring...

In August of 1806, both groups returned to the Mandan and Hidatsa settlement in North Dakota. It was the end of the journey for Sacagawea and her family. She had gone thousands of miles over 16 months. Now, it was time to say good-bye. The rest of the Corps continued on its way home.

Clark had grown very fond of little Jean Baptiste. When it was time to part, Clark offered to care for the boy when he was old enough to leave his mother. Clark promised to keep Jean Baptiste safe and send him to school. Three years later, Sacagawea and Charbonneau traveled to St. Louis. They visited Clark and left their son in his care.

Sacagawea, Charbonneau, and Jean Baptiste in Missouri

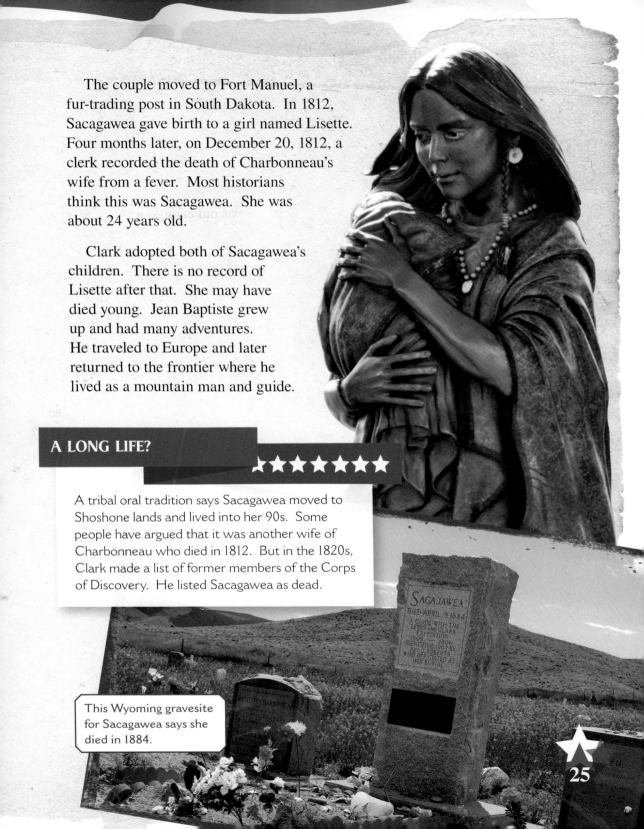

The couple moved to Fort Manuel, a fur-trading post in South Dakota. In 1812, Sacagawea gave birth to a girl named Lisette. Four months later, on December 20, 1812, a clerk recorded the death of Charbonneau's wife from a fever. Most historians think this was Sacagawea. She was about 24 years old.

Clark adopted both of Sacagawea's children. There is no record of Lisette after that. She may have died young. Jean Baptiste grew up and had many adventures. He traveled to Europe and later returned to the frontier where he lived as a mountain man and guide.

## A LONG LIFE?

A tribal oral tradition says Sacagawea moved to Shoshone lands and lived into her 90s. Some people have argued that it was another wife of Charbonneau who died in 1812. But in the 1820s, Clark made a list of former members of the Corps of Discovery. He listed Sacagawea as dead.

This Wyoming gravesite for Sacagawea says she died in 1884.

SACAJAWEA
DIED APRIL 9 1884
A GUIDE WITH THE
LEWIS AND CLARK
EXPEDITION
1805    1806
IDENTIFIED 1907 BY
REV J ROBERTS
WHO OFFICIATED AT
HER BURIAL

# A Legacy of Exploration

Lewis and Clark did not find the Northwest Passage. But in other ways, their expedition achieved its goals. They mapped a westward route along the Missouri and Columbia Rivers. They met many American Indian tribes. They recorded the geography and plant and animal life of the vast new territory. And they opened the way for Americans to move west.

Over the years, legends have grown about Sacagawea's role in the Corps of Discovery. Many people think she was Lewis and Clark's guide. Paintings and statues show her pointing the way westward. It is true that she helped guide the explorers through Shoshone lands. But she mainly served as an interpreter rather than a guide.

Still, Sacagawea had a key role to play. She endured hunger, cold, and hardship alongside the men. She gathered food and cared for the sick. Along the way, she ensured a peaceful welcome from tribes. She helped the Corps trade for horses to cross the mountains. In tough times, she showed poise and courage. The real woman who inspired the legend of Sacagawea was a true American trailblazer.

A Map of LEWIS AND CLARK'S Across the Western Por North America From the MISSISSIPPI TO THE PACIFIC By Order of the Executive of the UNITED STATES in 1804.5&6. Copied by Samuel Lewis from the Original Drawing of W. Clark.

## LARGER THAN LIFE

★★★★★

There are few facts we know about Sacagawea's life. Writers have created **myths** to fill the gaps. Some claim she had a romance with either Lewis or Clark or that she was a princess. But there is no evidence to support these claims.

1814 map of Lewis and Clark's expedition

Sacagawea speaks with Lewis and Clark.

# Map It!

One of Lewis and Clark's most important jobs was to draw maps of the territory they explored. Now, create your own map.

Draw a map of the United States. Draw the route the Corps of Discovery took. Mark important stops they made along the way. Use an online map as a reference. Write a caption explaining the importance of each place. Include these important stops:

- Hidatsa and Mandan settlement near what is now Washburn, North Dakota

- Great Falls, Montana, where they had to carry their boats

- Three Forks, Montana

- Fort Clatsop near what is now Astoria, Oregon

Lewis looks at the Rocky Mountains for the first time.

# Glossary

**band**—a group of people, usually smaller than a tribe

**corps**—an organized group of people involved in the same activity

**cradleboard**—a protective baby carrier worn on the back by American Indians

**culture**—the beliefs and ways of a group of people

**customs**—traditional behaviors or actions of a group of people

**enslaved**—forced to work without pay and without freedom

**expedition**—a journey to a new place by a group of people for a specific reason

**frontier**—an area where few people live

**historians**—people who write about or study history

**interpreter**—a person who translates words into another language

**lore**—traditional stories that relate to a particular place, subject, or group

**myths**—stories that are believed by many people but are not true

**settlement**—a place where people have come to live

**tepees**—cone-shaped tents that were used by American Indians as houses

**terrain**—land with a particular kind of physical features

**territory**—an area of land that is controlled by the government

**translate**—change from one language to another language

**tribe**—a group of people who have the same language, customs, and beliefs

# Index

# Your Turn!

## Sacagawea's Journal

    Lewis and Clark recorded new sights, sounds, and experiences in their journals.  They wrote about and drew new plants and animals that people in the United States had never seen before.  Their entries also taught us much of what we know about Sacagawea.  Imagine that Sacagawea kept a journal, too.  What might she have written about?  How might she have been feeling?  Write a journal entry that Sacagawea might have written during her time with Lewis and Clark.